Do Your Bit to Be Physically Fit!

Rebecca Sjonger

Crabtree Publishing Company
www.crabtreebooks.com

J
613.71
S6259

Author
Rebecca Sjonger

Publishing plan research and development
Reagan Miller

Editor
Reagan Miller

Proofreader
Crystal Sikkens

Consultant
Steve Sanders, Ed.D.,
Professor, Early Childhood Physical Activity,
University of South Florida

Design
Samara Parent

Photo research
Samara Parent

Production coordinator and prepress technician
Samara Parent

Print coordinator
Margaret Amy Salter

Photographs
istockphoto: (front cover), 21 (middle left and right)
Thinkstock: title page, p. 4, 5 (top), 6, 8 (right), 11 (bottom right), 16 (all), 17 (top and middle), 18 (bottom), 21 (top), 22 (both)
All other images by Shutterstock

Library and Archives Canada Cataloguing in Publication

Sjonger, Rebecca, author
    Do your bit to be physically fit! / Rebecca Sjonger.

(Healthy habits for a lifetime)
Includes index.
Issued in print and electronic formats.
ISBN 978-0-7787-1879-6 (bound).--ISBN 978-0-7787-1883-3 (paperback).--ISBN 978-1-4271-1624-6 (pdf).--ISBN 978-1-4271-1620-8 (html)

    1. Exercise--Juvenile literature. 2. Exercise for children--Juvenile literature. 3. Exercise--Health aspects--Juvenile literature. 4. Physical fitness--Juvenile literature. 5. Physical fitness for children--Juvenile literature. I. Title.

RA781.S6 2015   j613.7'1   C2015-903935-5
                                         C2015-903936-3

Library of Congress Cataloging-in-Publication Data

CIP available at Library of Congress

Crabtree Publishing Company

Printed in Canada/102015/IH20150821

www.crabtreebooks.com   1-800-387-7650

Copyright © **2016 CRABTREE PUBLISHING COMPANY**. All rights reserved. No part of this publication may be reproduced, stored in a retrieval system or be transmitted in any form or by any means, electronic, mechanical, photocopying, recording, or otherwise, without the prior written permission of Crabtree Publishing Company. In Canada: We acknowledge the financial support of the Government of Canada through the Canada Book Fund for our publishing activities.

Published in Canada
Crabtree Publishing
616 Welland Ave.
St. Catharines, Ontario
L2M 5V6

Published in the United States
Crabtree Publishing
PMB 59051
350 Fifth Avenue, 59th Floor
New York, New York 10118

Published in the United Kingdom
Crabtree Publishing
Maritime House
Basin Road North, Hove
BN41 1WR

Published in Australia
Crabtree Publishing
3 Charles Street
Coburg North
VIC 3058

Contents

Active for life

Running, jumping, swinging, and catching are **physical** skills we learn through play. We use these skills in activities all our lives—even as adults! Besides being fun, physical activity makes us feel good and gives us **energy**. What is your favorite way to get your body moving?

4

Making physical activity an important part of your day is a good **habit** to form. Being active will help you be healthy the rest of your life.

Being active is just one part of being healthy. You should also eat foods that are good for you, and get plenty of sleep.

Look for fun, active ways to spend time with your friends and family.

Body moves

Physical activity helps keep your body healthy. Being active makes your muscles and bones strong. It uses the energy you get from food. Fat is burned away instead of being stored in your body. Physical activity even helps your body fight off illnesses.

Your body works better when you are more active. The level of energy you have during the day increases, too. Being active even helps you sleep better at night.

Learning to balance your body is a skill that will help you with many activities.

Practice basic physical skills often and you will become better at them! Traveling skills include running and jumping. Controlling objects, such as a ball using different parts of your body, is another important skill.

Boost your brain

Physical activity is just as good for your brain as it is for your body! It affects how we feel. Being active helps us to be happier. Kids who are active are also more **confident**. They feel good about themselves.

How do you feel after you have been active?

Being active also helps kids do well in school. They think more clearly and focus better. They can remember more of what they learn. Students who are active before a test often get higher grades. Try it yourself! Ask your teacher if you could do your next test after a gym class.

EXAM #1

NAME: Amber

Answer:

1. A ✓
2. D ✓
3. B ✓
   C ✓
   A ✓

6. C ✓
7. D ✓
8. B ✓
   A ✓
9.
10. C

A+

Build endurance

Kids need at least 60 minutes of physical activity each day. Break up the hour into shorter chunks and move your body in different ways. Jumping rope, running, and swimming are all **aerobic** activities. You must move your arm or leg muscles in a steady rhythm to do them. These actions use a lot of **oxygen** and energy. Your heart beats faster. Your lungs must also work harder.

25 minutes
Swimming lessons

15 minutes
Ride bike to and from school

20 minutes
Practice skateboarding with friends

Aerobic activities build your body's **endurance**. This is how long you are able to do a physical activity. You must build up endurance over time. Doing too much too soon can hurt your body.

Drink plenty of water when you **sweat**. Avoid sugary sports drinks or juice. Water is all you need to keep your heart and muscles working well.

Strength training

Doing a mix of activities uses different muscles. You can help your muscles grow stronger by making them work harder. Use your own body weight to build your muscles. For example, activities such as running and kicking a ball strengthen your leg muscles. Strength training also improves the endurance of your muscles.

Kids should not lift weights. You could injure your muscles or bones. Try climbing on playground equipment instead.

Skipping is another activity that can help build strong bones.

Bone strength is important for kids' growing bodies. When you run or jump, you hit the ground with your feet. The impact with the ground makes your feet and leg bones work harder and get stronger. Fun ways to build bone strength include playing hopscotch, tennis, or basketball.

Bendy bodies

Being flexible is very important in dancing and karate.

Being **flexible** helps you with all physical activities. The more freely your body can bend and stretch, the more flexible you are. Many kids stay flexible by moving, reaching, and stretching as they play. You can become more flexible by doing activities that stretch your muscles.

14

How flexible are you? Stand up and then bend down and try to touch your toes. Keep your knees straight but loose. Did you find it easy or hard to stretch your back and leg muscles?

Get your 60!

Many kids spend over seven hours in front of a computer, television, or video game console each day! Limit yourself to two hours or less. That will leave you time to try a new physical activity! Doing something new keeps being active exciting.

Here are some ideas for how to get your 60 minutes of activity each day:

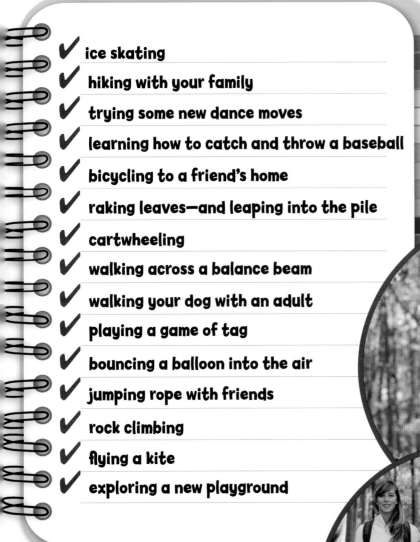

- ✔ ice skating
- ✔ hiking with your family
- ✔ trying some new dance moves
- ✔ learning how to catch and throw a baseball
- ✔ bicycling to a friend's home
- ✔ raking leaves—and leaping into the pile
- ✔ cartwheeling
- ✔ walking across a balance beam
- ✔ walking your dog with an adult
- ✔ playing a game of tag
- ✔ bouncing a balloon into the air
- ✔ jumping rope with friends
- ✔ rock climbing
- ✔ flying a kite
- ✔ exploring a new playground

Make time each day for improving your physical skills with the help of an adult.

Take action!

These pages give you some physical activity tips:

> **Slowly build up your activity level.**

> **Create your own action plan that lists how you will get 60 minutes or more of activity each day.**

> **Get your family and friends to join you. Cheer one another on as you try your best!**

18

You should be able to say at least a few words while you are being active. If you can still sing, try a little harder. Slow down if you are breathless or unable to talk.

You are getting a good workout when you sweat and your heart beats faster. Be sure to drink plenty of water.

Track your daily activities so you know how much time you spend being active.

Remember that healthy eating and sleeping well are also important habits to form.

Obstacle course

An **obstacle** course is a fun way to work on your endurance and strength. It can even develop your flexibility and balance. Look at the sample course in the picture on the right. Each station uses your body in different ways.

Create your own obstacle course!
Plan stations that:

✔ get your heart beating faster and your lungs working harder to improve endurance

✔ work your muscles to make them stronger

✔ have your feet hitting the ground to strengthen bones

✔ make your body bend and stretch

✔ challenge you to balance in different positions without falling over

My Obstacle Course

Start

1. crab-walking

2. hopscotch

3. balance beam

4. pylon zig-zag

Show what you know!

How much physical activity do kids need each day?

a. 10 minutes

b. 30 minutes

c. 60 minutes

d. 90 minutes

Look at Jack's day. Is he getting at least 60 minutes of physical activity? What changes could he make to be more physically active?

Jack's Day

▸ Get a drive to and from school	**2 minutes**
▸ Read book during recess	**20 minutes**
▸ Work up a sweat during gym	**30 minutes**
▸ Play video games after school	**60 minutes**
▸ Watch television after dinner	**60 minutes**

Jack could ride his bike to school!

Answer: Try to be physically active for at least 60 minutes every day.

22

Learning more

Websites

Find out how to be physically active and have fun at:
http://kidshealth.org/kid/stay_healthy/fit/what_time.html

Learn how physical activity helps your body at:
http://kidshealth.org/kid/stay_healthy/fit/work_it_out.html

This site has tips for getting started with a physical activity plan and more—not just for girls!
www.girlshealth.gov/fitness/started/index.html

Books

Atha, Antony. *Fitness for Young People: Step-by-step*. Rosen Central, 2010.

Doeden, Matt. *Stay fit! : How you can get in shape*. Lerner, 2009.

Kajander, Rebecca. *Be Fit, Be Strong, Be You*. Free Spirit, 2010.

Rockwell, Lizzy. *The Busy Body Book: A Kid's Guide to Fitness*. Random House, 2008.

Most websites with addresses that end in ".org" or ".gov" have current information that you can trust.

23

Words to know

aerobic [air-OH-bik] adjective Activity that uses extra oxygen and makes the heart and lungs stronger

confident [KON-fi-dent] adjective Believing in your own abilities

endurance [in-DUR-ince] noun The ability to do something over a long period

energy [en-ER-gee] noun The body or mind's ability to do work

flexible [FLEK-si-bel] adjective Able to bend easily

habit [HAB-it] noun The way someone usually acts or thinks

obstacle [OB-sti-kel] noun An object you have to go around or over

oxygen [AK-si-jen] noun A part of the air that people need to breathe to survive

physical [FI-zi-kel] adjective Related to the body

sweat [swet] verb To lose moisture from the body through the skin

A *noun* is a person, place, or thing.
A *verb* expresses an action.
An *adjective* tells us what something is like.

Index